Reading Girl

poems by

Elizabeth Paul

Finishing Line Press
Georgetown, Kentucky

Reading Girl

Copyright © 2016 by Elizabeth Paul
ISBN 978-1-63534-059-4 First Edition
All rights reserved under International and Pan-American Copyright Conventions.
No part of this book may be reproduced in any manner whatsoever without written permission from the publisher, except in the case of brief quotations embodied in critical articles and reviews.

ACKNOWLEDGMENTS

Publisher: Leah Maines

Editor: Christen Kincaid

Cover Art: Elizabeth Paul

Author Photo: Stanislav Miachkov

Cover Design: Elizabeth Maines

Printed in the USA on acid-free paper.
Order online: www.finishinglinepress.com
also available on amazon.com

Author inquiries and mail orders:
Finishing Line Press
P. O. Box 1626
Georgetown, Kentucky 40324
U. S. A.

Table of Contents

Harmony in Red, 1908, Henri Matisse 1
The Piano Lesson, 1916, Henri Matisse 2
Girl Reading, 1905-06, Henri Matisse 3
Japanese Mask, 1950, Henri Matisse 4
Girl with Tulips, 1910, Henri Matisse 5
Still Life with Sleeping Woman, 1940, Henri Matisse 6
Odalisque with a Tambourine, 1925-1926, Henri Matisse 7
Laurette with a White Blouse, 1916, Henri Matisse 8
Reading Girl, 1922, Henri Matisse 9
Zulma, 1950, Henri Matisse 10
Still Life with Geraniums, 1910, Henri Matisse 11
Two Figures Reclining in a Landscape, 1921, Henri Matisse 12
Odalisque, 1923, Henri Matisse 13
Tahiti Landscape, 1931, Henri Matisse 14
Music, 1939, Henri Matisse 15
Pianist and Still-Life, 1924, Henri Matisse 16
Woman at the Fountain, 1917, Henri Matisse 17
Interior in Yellow, 1948, Henri Matisse 18
The Artist's Family, 1912, Henri Matisse 19
Marguerite, 1906, Henri Matisse 20
The Daisies, 1939, Henri Matisse 21
Two Girls in a Yellow and Red Interior, 1947, Henri Matisse 22
Annelies, White Tulips and Anemones, 1944, Henri Matisse 23
Index of Artworks and Locations 24

For Doug and Roselyn

Harmony in Red, **1908, Henri Matisse**

The meniscus of a fainter orange or paler lemon is a concession of essences to take up space and draw lines of viscosity against their crystal containers. She is held in a pattern of wild domesticity, the rebellion latent in refinement, spring on the ground when there is still snow in the trees. Our scarlet houses, pale on the horizon, burn in crimson containment of themselves.

The Piano Lesson, 1916, Henri Matisse

Sometimes you have to subdue the mind to free it for other things. So says the briefcase. Meanwhile the boy is like a note in a measure, trapped between black lines and scrolls and waiting for music to happen. He is in that exacting stage of learning to count. The music isn't in him yet—in his hands or his head. It is at best a decorative touch, a green potential in his periphery. Only the beat is slowly colonizing his mind through its indefatigable indifference. In the takeover his head becomes a metronome and a grotesque decapitation is accomplished. The clacking discipline turns his audience-mother into a faceless, earless watcher—daft, demure and hollow. So there is another casualty. It's just a phase, but things will never be the same.

Girl Reading, **1905-06, Henri Matisse**

Her head never feels as heavy as in an afternoon of reading—there is a somnolence, an oppressive focus and abstention from the day. Across and down the pages she tunnels while everything around her resents her inattention. The neglected pitcher trades bitter thoughts with the slighted table cloth adorned for delight. Apples and pears like preoccupied pigeons scavenge ever further from the moment of ripeness. Proud flower vases talk among themselves, making sure to be overheard now and again. The pictures on the wall hang out of reach, lucid only in denial that they had ever been hers. How is such distraction to be borne?

Japanese Mask, **1950, Henri Matisse**

Out the window the lake is in one of its moods. You see eyes welling with tears but think you shouldn't say anything—think one more word might be too many.

In a studio apartment a man paints from his window. A failure man, former salesman, resume writer, and family castaway. Thinks: *there is more there through this here.* Thinks: *always, through history, the snail.*

Girl with Tulips, **1910, Henri Matisse**

Spring-scapes reach implausible endings, in soul conceived and soil cradled. Rocking, swinging, orbiting, bending. Belts, buckles, cuffs and collars. Out of round things come tulips—straight up—boldly into embrace: blue and gold, sun and sky, the interlocking fingers of energy and serenity.

Still Life with Sleeping Woman, **1940, Henri Matisse**

The plants are the dream. Floating. Meandering. As dreams do. Vascular hands become reptiles become aquarium fronds, trees, green beans, dance, gestures, jungle play of petioles, tentacles, lace. The plants, like visions, awake in her sleep, fill the room and hover without root or reason.

The chair is the ironic anchor. Everything needs its bashfulness, its pacific testament to uncertainty. The chair is the bird at the window of being whose small noises penetrate the dream with their bright unseen adjacency. The chair is the frankness of form that lets us ignore things and see.

The amphora is the woman poured out of the mysterious richness pitchers imply. A bare neck and curve of shoulder. A coiled form slumped in somnolent cascade contained by time's liquid table, the weightlessness of an afternoon.

The fruits are the woman's gifts, her kin, and her confidantes. The mind's bright arc of treasure. A beaded distillation, sound of sunlight, and play of surrender. The fruits are the ability of things to transcend themselves. The fruits are mostly everywhere.

The window is the problem. The shout, the blank, the rest of the world, the awaking without which nothing would float. The woman might be dead, the whole scene hopeless without its fire rim and congress with fruit. The window is the eye, the way everything can be everything else.

Odalisque with a Tambourine, **1925-1926, Henri Matisse**

What a bliss to be one's own wholesome self, elliptical and in tune with a candid room. To be red-bold and table-steady—useless of words but essential, a consistent sign. To master your posture and play your perfect part with gold-striped confidence and blue inhibition.

Laurette with a White Blouse, **1916, Henri Matisse**

A modest Salacia, goddess of sea and springs, was Laurette with a white blouse: black visions and voyages in her eyes, ripples in her hands, inflections in her hair. Fathoms, tides and crossings the plying of her mind. Too much time to contemplate a life.

Reading Girl, **1922, Henri Matisse**

Arranged like a bouquet, quiet object of admiration, on the petals of your blouse plays the light, reading girl. Your mind's movement is stilled by a plate of untouched grapes. You sit at a lonely table absent of cause or consequence, stuck in an impasse of agreeable adjacency.

Zulma, 1950, Henri Matisse

Zulma took a bus from the zoo. Zulma took a swim in the community pool. She bought stationary at the Hallmark store and joined the millinery society of West Hartford. She gave up one hand and renounced her animal nature, but it was enough. Now she stares with her no-eyes and steadies herself against the furniture. Zulma studies in hotel lobbies, apprenticed to fake plants, flower arrangements, and gold framed mirrors. She is chilled and a little nauseous—sometimes her knuckles scrape the ground. But Zulma holds it together.

Still Life with Geraniums, **1910, Henri Matisse**

You didn't think you'd ever have the whole picture, did you? If you are frustrated, maybe that's good—an alternative to delusion, believing too little in the world's capacity to surprise. What wonders you've been missing, like someone turning from street performers, embarrassed by their apparent vulnerability. It's hard for you to look at the geraniums that hide themselves in full view.

Two Figures Reclining in a Landscape, **1921, Henri Matisse**

From the carousel of his infirmity, he saw a garbage can world, a cafeteria tray on which someone had played with his food—rice, refried beans, and strawberry jam, mustard, sugar, peas and carrots, chicken fingers and butterscotch pudding. It was irresistible. He would have lapped the horses to pile on something more.

Odalisque, **1923, Henri Matisse**

Hard to imagine that being all those lines could feel as dull as sitting. Did her side go numb, her arms ache? Her hair is like a tide or a hunted creature too beautiful to be safe, too naturally lustrous and not even knowing it. Did she feel the rhythm of her body? Could she sense the pattern of her flesh any more than the divan? In a room with window shades closed to the day, he tamed another creature to prove it wild.

Tahiti Landscape, **1931, Henri Matisse**

All the trees are shivering, alone and cold in the company of each other, posturing, awkward, and feigning indifference to their hearts on their sleeves, their yellow heads in the breeze. Eyes on the blue because everything else is emergency broadcasting system. Eyes on the blue—it's the only purchase in this piebald panic of rootlessness.

Music, 1939, Henri Matisse

It was a day of progress enamored with the signs of itself. Talented ladies lounged like common giants. It was a circus moment, a paradise parade. More organic things would step in line or make way. It was a time for long legs, broad shoulders, and breasts round as fruit, capacious hands, short hair, and faces like jotted notes.

Pianist and Still-Life, 1924, Henri Matisse

It doesn't take much—just an attention to what's nearest—to notice how precious this place is, like a dollhouse anticipating our humanity. The black staves of sheet music, the grain of a piano's wood, the brass studs along the base of an armchair. We are living in miniature. The whole inner world of the woman fits in a straight back chair and pours into the piano and out with the music, across the wall in triple octaves, arching like a celebrated entrance to the room in which she sits. There is nowhere else to go. Our biggest dreams can't contain the sheen of pink satin or exceed the fullness of a single whole note.

Woman at the Fountain, 1917, **Henri Matisse**

Faceless, nameless, a little bit there as well as here, the woman at the fountain is more presence than flesh, a hovering, ghosted about-ness. She is arriving from or leaving for a big black tare in the day. A dopey-headed liminality, she is a guillotine ghoul of doubtful opacity, this society lady with a strand of pearls. Her pastel kingdom is a squall of curtailed spontaneity—the muddy banks of a darksome source.

Interior in Yellow, **1948, Henri Matisse**

There are doors passing like trains through the room, and everyone is trying to act natural. It's such a long shot between beginning and end, and everyone is trying to act natural. There's an entrance and an exit with nothing in between. Everybody knows it, and everybody is trying to act natural.

Wall, says the wall. *Wall, wall, wall.*

With legs, says the plant stand, *I hold up the plant.*

Look, look, look at our delightful green stripes and our spherical forms, cry the watermelons.

They are all so desperate that they are crawling out of their skins.

It's hard for the chair to bear this yellow interior. In the corner it partakes of the portal and hears its cobalt caterwaul of points and needles. It is nearing its breaking point, about to stand up and storm off. But the table is pleased with itself and with everyone. In the center of things, it can hardly afford to feel otherwise.

The Artist's Family, **1912, Henri Matisse**

He always cared more for the board than for the checkers, more for the pattern than for the pawns. What was anything worth if there wasn't some eternity in it? What couldn't stand to be shaved down a bit—head or toes? He didn't care who won, only that there was diagonal advance. He didn't care for kings, only that the pieces clacked. Black duty, red rivalry, jaundice dreariness. What mattered was how they hovered in the living room.

Marguerite, **1906, Henri Matisse**

Straight-jacketed into a dress like a building, its high lace collar a chimney to the jaw. Her head a bobble, ceramic dish, death mask. Hair untenable, propped up of green. Black eyes like holes, coals, birds' heads with sharp beaks. Snakes on her brow, nose like a swan, mouth a sunset lake in the landscape of her face.

The Daisies, **1939, Henri Matisse**

Stand at the gate barking at intruders. They know who belongs. Six lemons covetable as canaries, the nouveau riche. The lady in red giggling, posturing, stalwart as a bison. The ancient amphora, overqualified and swollen with opinions. A famous painting basking in immortality. The daisies smelled the dark on them and let them in.

Two Girls in a Yellow and Red Interior, **1947, Henri Matisse**

It wasn't because half the walls were red and the table was red and the pomegranates on the platter were red nor because the other half of the walls were yellow and the sides of the table were yellow and the roses in the vase were yellow nor because they lived in a house with a cafeteria mentality that the sisters' skins turned purple, but because the tree at the window wasn't right in the head, and they lived in sympathy with their surroundings.

Annelies, White Tulips and Anemones, **1944, Henri Matisse**

Here, at last, a woman not hunched over a book or absorbed in thought but sitting up straight in a tall chair at a wide desk. Annelies caught in the middle of something, looking back. For once, the painter confronted. At least one of her eyes is more than a mere mark. Even the anemones can see. Annelies puts clothes on in the morning and takes care of her hands. The tulips turn their heads. She turns the pages.

Index of Artworks and Locations

Visit *elizabethsgpaul.com* to view these paintings and cut-outs online.

Annelies, White Tulips and Anemones, 1944, Henri Matisse: Honolulu Museum of Art

The Artist's Family, 1912, Henri Matisse: The State Hermitage Museum

The Daisies, 1939, Henri Matisse: Art Institute of Chicago

Girl Reading, 1905-06, Henri Matisse: Museum of Modern Art

Girl with Tulips, 1910, Henri Matisse: The State Hermitage Museum

Harmony in Red, 1908, Henri Matisse: The State Hermitage Museum

Interior in Yellow, 1948, Henri Matisse: Musée National d'Art Moderne, Georges Pompidou Center

Japanese Mask, 1950, Henri Matisse: Private Collection

Laurette with a White Blouse, 1916, Henri Matisse: Eykyn Maclean Gallery

Marguerite, 1906, Henri Matisse: Marion Smooke Collection

Music, 1939, Henri Matisse: Albright-Knox Art Gallery

Odalisque, 1923, Henri Matisse: Stedelijk Museum

Odalisque with a Tambourine, 1925-1926, Henri Matisse: Museum of Modern Art

Pianist and Still-Life, 1924, Henri Matisse: Kunst Museum Berne

The Piano Lesson, 1916, Henri Matisse: Museum of Modern Art

Reading Girl, 1922, Henri Matisse: Musée d'art moderne de Troyes

Still Life with Geraniums, 1910, Henri Matisse: Pinakothek der Moderne

Still Life with Sleeping Woman, 1940, Henri Matisse: National Gallery of Art

Tahiti Landscape, 1931, Henri Matisse: Private Collection

Two Figures Reclining in a Landscape, 1921, Henri Matisse: The Barnes Foundation

Two Girls in a Yellow and Red Interior, 1947, Henri Matisse: The Barnes Foundation

Woman at the Fountain, 1917, Henri Matisse: Private Collection

Zulma, 1950, Henri Matisse: Statens Museum for Kunst

Elizabeth Paul studied art and literature at The Evergreen State College and continued in an interdisciplinary vein at the University of Virginia where she earned an MA in English in the American Studies Program. She holds an MFA in creative writing from the Vermont College of Fine Arts, and her creative and critical work has appeared in *River Teeth, Cold Mountain Review, Weave Magazine,* and *Assay.*

Elizabeth taught college writing and literature for six years, working with students from around the world. Prior to teaching, she wrote, edited, and designed content for the Library of Congress's educational website, The Learning Page. For two years she served as a Peace Corps education volunteer in Kyrgyzstan where she met and married her husband.

Her interests in culture, art, language, and nature have taken her to Mexico, East Africa, Western Europe, Russia, and Turkey. Elizabeth teaches ESOL and writing in the Washington, D.C. area. To contact her or to learn more about *Reading Girl* and the art on which it is based visit www.elizabethsgpaul.com.

www.ingramcontent.com/pod-product-compliance
Lightning Source LLC
LaVergne TN
LVHW041517070426
835507LV00012B/1625